the gen Z's

Rags to Riches Handbook

Jake P L Jones

CONTENTS

ACKNOWLEDGMENTS

Many thanks to all those who made this book a reality. I want to give a special thanks to both my parents and grandparents, who have supported me through my journey and allowed me to pursue my passions.

INTRODUCTION

Yes, before you ask I am a member of generation Z meaning I was born between the years 1995-2009, 2002 to be exact, and in just 5 months have created enough wealth to be considered in the 1%. Right now, is the best time in history for someone in my generation to start building wealth, the opportunities are endless because of the internet. Anybody can get the advice of billionaires from YouTube, people can form a company in just 5 minutes and a teenager can use his birthday money to create a fortune. Something that just 20 years ago would have seemed impossible. Ambition is a great asset to have but without the knowledge to act on it can be crippling. I feel I have a purpose to pass on my knowledge to other young people who can use my experience to better their financial lives and to simply have more money, something everybody wants but only a few will gain the financial education to do so and even fewer at a young age.

Money was always important to me growing up since I thought money makes you more independent and gives you freedom from your parents. I was unhappy with my home life and just felt stuck in an average suburban area, I wanted more out of life but lacked the confidence to approach people for jobs and even advice. I was always a quiet kid with relatively good grades, would rush home to play Xbox with my friends after school and go out when I could. I had wanted to be a doctor since the age of 14 so went to college and studied my A-levels. It was in my second year of college when I was bored at home (as most gen Z's usually are) that I searched the infamous 'highest-paying jobs' on my laptop. Stockbroker jumped out at me. This one google search started my obsession with trading on the stock market and ultimately started my financial rollercoaster that would follow that year. All other interests were put aside, and I started my financial education at the age of 18.

On my 18th birthday, the 1st of March 2020, I started at just £400 and achieved some extraordinary returns. I am going to take you through my 5-month journey and show you step by step how I did it. No bullshit. All you need is an internet connection and a phone, something everybody has. In the gen Z's Rags to Riches handbook, I walk you through my ridiculous trading experiences in March. I tell you the do's and don'ts of personal finance in April and tell you how to invest for the long-term in May. June, I share my principles while confronting some immoral people. Then I walk you through how I launched my company in July and how anybody can use my concepts to increase their wealth, even a gen Z. I feel as though in my 5 months as a trader, investor, and director of a company I have had my fair share of both good and bad experiences. This generation Z's handbook is not just about how to go from rags to riches but also how to avoid losing money, such as when I relied too heavily on technology and was misled by an account manager. There will be more on my worst decisions in chapter 2 where I explored what newfound wealth could buy and why you should live like your poor. You do not need any special skills or need to have a rocket high IQ to become 'rich', it is just a matter of timing and using the tools I will show you later in the handbook. Tools such as using leverage to achieve higher profits but more on that in chapter 1. As a general rule, I believe a person can achieve their version of financial success when preparation meets opportunity and for me, my first opportunity came in March 2020.

Disclaimer: I am not a financial advisor

CHAPTER 1: MARCH

THE TRADING BONANZA

The coronavirus hit the whole world in March, the pandemic shut the economy down and the world almost stood still for a month while the government figured out what to do. I, on the other hand, was elated I didn't need to sit my exams later that year. My college closed in late February and I stayed home for my birthday, March the 1st. It was uneventful, I received my modest £400 and funded my trading account. During January and February, I had been using a demo account with fake money, intending to make 1% of my total balance per day. Having a good track record on the rising market of February I decided it was time for me to step up and use a real account after my birthday. I risked my £400, younger people can usually handle more risk than older generations. I am a strong believer in 'risk it until you make it' but be sure to put aside enough money to cover your expenses. If I lost my £400 then my life would have been no different than before since my parents covered my expenses so I welcomed the risk.

March the 2nd came around and the market opened at 8 am. I woke up 1 hour before to look at related news and to decide which stocks to trade, I decided on the French index (a collection of French stocks). This was my first trading day so I wanted to start strong and achieve a small profit to boost my confidence. I had spent two months planning out this day and in my mind, nothing could go wrong. I sat down in my bedroom and opened my account. This was it, I was finally about to start making money but in typical gen Z fashion I never even thought about what could go wrong.

8:00 am struck, my palms were sweaty and I suddenly became very hot. On the morning of March the 2nd, my anxiety levels were high. This near physical meltdown was not because I was using my £400 but because I was using leverage on my account. Leverage uses the brokers (the websites) money and adds the money to your initial deposit. The leverage on my account was a staggering 1:100 meaning I was trading with £40,000 from using my tiny deposit. Without leverage, my profits would have been 100 times less throughout the month, if you are starting small then leverage is a great way to propel your profits but with one wrong trade, a one-way ticket to losing your deposit. My account was also margined which meant if I lost too much money then I would not be in debt to the brokers and would only lose my initial deposit. The Limited downside with unlimited upside seemed like a perfect deal. In hindsight it was and the profits I produced in March would prove it. In a world where the average amount of savings is only £1000 leverage is king.

My first two days of trading went better than planned and in those two days I had made more than my parents had made by working their jobs, I felt rich. I didn't know another gen Z who earned that much in such a short amount of time. For the first time in my life, I felt content and it was down to how much money I had, I loved money. On the 3rd day of March (my second trading day) I had been learning about puts and calls. Buying a call is when you bet on the instrument (stock or index) increasing in value. If you buy a put you bet the instrument falling in value. Puts and calls move much faster in value than normal stocks meaning that the profits or losses are much higher, they are a very risky game to play, luckily I was a risk-taker. By this time the coronavirus was getting much worse around the globe and I was looking online at the news. I saw one headline saying 'the economy will collapse' a headline filled with dread. I did the maths and decided the stock market was likely to follow. What I now consider as a defining moment in my life I used my leveraged money to buy £35,000 worth of puts (after leverage) before the market closed around 9 pm, betting the market would fall the next day. The market opened at 1 am, I was asleep and probably dreaming about the next £1000 I hoped to make that week.

7 am, I was awake. I checked the notifications on my phone, a ritual for any gen Z when they wake up. There was a figure on my screen that read 'Put +750%'. I logged into my account and saw that my account was up by thousands. To my pure joy, the market had plunged by hundreds of points. I am not proud of the event that followed, running downstairs, and proceeding to do what can only be described as a kind of jiggle, nobody should be seen doing a jiggle. I called my friend George (who I often conferred with about stocks) to tell him the magnitude of my profits.

We both decided I had a big decision to make, either hold my position and risk losing my profit or cash out the money. It was a decision that was going to change my life and I needed to make it fast. After a one-hour phone call, I decided it was not worth the risk and had made up my mind. I was going to cash out. During the call, I had made another £200. I said 'f*ck it, I'm holding'.

I have never been a religious person, even though I am from a Cristian family. If I felt that God was ever looking down on me, it was over the events that transpired on the 4th and 5th of march. All-day I had been checking my laptop and phone for new notifications on my position. I had to stop myself from looking. My screen time on the 4th of March was only 33 minutes, unheard of for a teenager. Puts usually last less than one month then the put will expire, I could potentially hold this put for a month. How bad was the market going to get? This was the question I asked myself over and over. The gen Z's Rags to Riches handbook teaches you how to take advantage of these extreme circumstances through my own experiences. The morning of March the 5th was an experience I would never forget.

I finally plucked up the courage to look at my account before trying to sleep, I was in profit by a few hundred and decided to add some of my profit to my position, nearly half. I had increased my risk, even more, looking back this was a great decision but at the time I was in fight or flight. I was in chemical overload and my mental state was deteriorating. I checked my position a few minutes later, the market was falling at a fast rate. Sleep was no longer an option. The market closed at 10 pm and was going to open on my brokerage account at 1 am. I sat through what felt like the longest 3 hours of my life. My clock eventually showed 00:58, 00:59, and finally 01:00. I looked hesitantly at my phone and saw the notification 'Put +1000%'. The Dow index (overall sum of the market) fell by 970 points later that day and the USA index (which I was basing my put on) fell by over 1000. What investors considered a freak event and an imminent market crash had given me a total profit of nearly £4000 in the space of a few hours, I was way past my parent's salary for the week. Needless to say, I cashed out.

Over 5 days, my wealth increased by just shy off 5000%. That is an average of 1000% per day. Spectacular returns. I was once again in a state of elation and felt nothing in the world could stop me, slowly getting more and more arrogant. I hadn't told my family about my newfound wealth, the only person I had told was my friend George who I fully trusted and so I was just acting normal in front of them. Even though inside I could hardly contain my joy. I was, however, paying the toll for being what I would consider a 'nervous wreck' for the past 2 days, trading made me physically and mentally exhausted. I slept through the 6th of March missing the end of the trading week, it was a welcomed break.

Withdrawing half my profits from my account was also a nerve-racking experience, I was used to being tech-savvy but doubt started to creep in and my anxiety returned. Due to this, I decided to move away from put and calls since they were much riskier than trading individual stocks. I also lowered my leverage from 1:100 to 1:20 however that still meant I was trading with after leverage £100,000 if I wanted a margin. When I worked out the figure after leverage I burst out laughing, it all seemed very surreal but I saw a problem. With the huge sum I was now trading with it made it very easy to lose my profit I had left in my account to trade with. That weekend I had a reality check and realised I was unbelievably lucky to make such a huge return in the first place and now using about half my profit to trade with I said 'screw it', something every gen Z has said at least once before doing something outrageous.

The weekend of the 7th and 8th of March was a weekend I used to re-cooperate and relax. I felt as though I was living in a dream. A part of me still wanted more, it just wasn't enough. I think my personality gives me a constant feeling of discontent which is a blessing and a curse because it gives me more drive but I feel I will always be working. I knew I needed to change my mental state if I wanted to carry on trading and making money. A lesson I only truly learned later in the year after a huge loss later in the month but we'll get to that. The 9th of March was dull, I endlessly searched through hundreds of stocks looking for the right opportunity. On this day I decided to go for a walk around dinner and I thought about the companies near where I lived, there were Nando's, Tesco, McDonalds and finally Cineworld. A great social hub and the best place to catch the new Marvel film. I looked at the stock on my account and saw it selling for £1.00 per share after a relatively good day for the company. Surely there was no way Cineworld could last in a pandemic world? This was my next opportunity, around 3 pm I decided to short Cineworld with my friend George with his position considerably smaller than mine but after leverage still enough to make a great profit. When you short a stock you bet the stock will lose value, they are like puts but less risky. It was a trade based only of common sense. The handbook shows you how to use common sense to make money, I was doing nothing special here just using initiative. We waited patiently all day, I was down by a few thousand by the close of the market. When trading you need to get acquainted with being at a loss due to spread, this is the difference between the buy and sell value. This usually puts you at a small loss whenever you open a position.

George was baffled, how could a company that was about to close down for months still be having good days on the stock market. I will admit being nervous that night, I did not want to lose my remaining profit in the account. I even considered closing my position, potentially losing thousands in the space of a few hours. Holding my nerve was hard and I awaited the following day anxiously.

The 10th of March arrived, I woke up from a restless sleep and once again called George as we both waited for the market to open. We made a joke about this day calling it 'judgement day'. For me, if this trade went wrong I would have stopped trading, taken my winnings, and called it a day. While I was making coffee, the fuel of most gen Z's, the market opened and Cineworld's marker shot down the screen. My hunch had paid off, the negative losses turned positive, each time I refreshed my account I made another thousand. George and I were amazed and probably more relieved. By using common sense and my love for movies I had made another great return and the number was still climbing. Once again I had the decision of holding or cashing out. I cashed out and altogether on the morning had made a 1000% return on my initial amount, me and George even talked about renting a Lamborghini, jokingly of course. I could not drive but it was still a nice feeling knowing I could afford to rent one.

George, on the other hand, decided to hold his position, a brave move that he would come to regret in the following week.

The first 10 days of March are the most smooth sailing days in the whole of this handbook, I look back and savour these 10 days, practically every stock in that period fell in value, even stocks such as apple. After March I learned not to get to high on the good times because bad times will always arrive. This is important for anybody who achieves a big boost in wealth in such a short amount of time but for me, I was not ready. I was a ticking time bomb.

I was walking on clouds for the week that followed, somehow I felt as though I deserved the money I made because of my two months on the demo account. Who is to say who deserves what? I knew deep down I was just lucky that my birthday was the 1st of March, meaning I could legally trade stocks from then on. The timing was everything, still I felt I was the next Warren Buffet. For those unaware of him, he has been called the father of investing. Ironically he does not agree with trading in short periods, at the time I had no idea. Over the next ten days I lowered my leverage to 1:5, I made consistent profits and life was all sunshine and rainbows.

I still had not told my family about the past 20 days, they did not even know I traded since I had been very discreet. Was now the right time to tell them? I decided to say that 'money was very important to me. Sound redundant, I know. That was all they needed to know, of course, I did not tell them how much but it was good enough for my conscience. I later found out they thought I was joking. As a child I had an awkward relationship with my parents, I felt they were too simple and in turn, they thought I was just 'of an age'. Every gen Z has experienced this statement and I still find it very infuriating which is why I tried to keep my home life and financial life separate. I was gradually getting more frustrated with my family and people I interacted with, my amygdala (the part of the brain which controls emotions) was taking over in conversations. As a trader, I acted similar to a robot. Emotions affected decision making and in trading, one wrong decision can be fatal. Training your brain to recognise when your amygdala is taking over can be invaluable, it makes you a more rational person. Giving you better relationships and leading to better overall decision making in life. You can look at yourself objectively and by doing this you can see which areas of your life need improvement. I would learn this the hard way because, in late March, my amygdala had completely taken over.

On the 23rd of March, I decided to trade oil, later in the handbook you see me have a great time with oil, with it being my last ever trade. This day was just not the right time, however. I was used to trading when the market was crashing or at least when the overall market was underperforming. The oil demand had slowed down dramatically by late March and it was reflected in the price. Oil had dropped by 50% in value over the past 23 days. To me, as a profit-hungry gen Z, it looked as though it was my textbook style. I had two options: either open a short position on an oil index or buy a put. Either would be betting on oil losing value but a put would be much riskier with the potential for a higher reward. In the handbook you see were timing can work in your favour for example in the first few weeks of March, you also see where timing can be your worst enemy. It is important to note that the market is a machine and does not care about your feelings. Happy or sad, it owes you nothing. I decided to go for a short position, which I hoped to hold for two days. I opened the position around 8 pm on the 23rd and waited it out. My position size was around a quarter of my total profit, which after leverage equated to a sizeable £20,000. I had a lot riding on this. Before I continue I need to explain (for those who don't know) what a dead cat bounce is, in relation to the market. When an instrument is losing value or in extreme circumstances crashing, the instrument can have a small surge on its way down. During a crash, the surges tend to be quite large. As for me, I shorted oil at the lowest possible point. A day before the 'dead cat bounce'. I was about to realise what it felt like to lose and to lose big.

The 24th of March rolled around, I was down £200 before the market closed, a poor start. I stayed optimistic because I had logic on my side, more and more people were staying at home. Surely oil was going to lose its value? As I explained earlier in the chapter I was trading with a margin on my account, if I lost enough money the trade would close and would count as a loss. The oil index opened at 8 am, I was running (I often run when stressed) but I had brought my phone so then I had to close the trade. My margin was at half the position size therefore my risk was the same as my margin. I was in the latter part of my run when I received a text. A margin alert had never happened to me before, it had always gone relatively smooth sailing when I traded and I also did not know that they alerted me by text. When I received the text I was blissfully unaware that I had just lost money. As a gen Z I was used to getting what seemed like a million notifications on my phone, I knew the sound of my brokerage and the sound of a text message. Thinking nothing of it I finished my run. As I finished it started to rain heavily, fitting for the situation. I looked at my phone while stretching and saw the text message. My heart sank and I was head in hands. I had just lost £3,000 in 12 hours. In other words, I had just lost more than a person's average monthly salary, my mind was thinking about what I could have used the money for. I hid away for the rest of the day in my room, if somebody had tried to talk to me I would have exploded and my amygdala would have been doing the talking (more accurately shouting). My mind had shifted from picturing me in a Lamborghini to me banging my head against my bedroom wall.....repeatedly.

That night I went for a walk around my area, to a nearby lake. My thoughts were very negative, after two hours of walking I decided to stop trading. I was going to take a week off and on the 25th of March withdrew my remaining balance. I had taken a hit but how could I complain? Trading had changed my life, it gave me the money I dreamed of. There was just one problem, what to do with it.

Summary of chapter 1:

Trading on the stock market is a great way to use leverage and achieve higher profits. I was trading in an extreme circumstance, such as a market crash. Other opportunities will come along in the future and trading stocks can be a great way to capitalise on these rare events. I recommend using a demo account before using your capital, just as I did. To start trading stocks is an easy process, simply search 'trading brokerages'.

Once you are adjusted to the workings of your brokerage and trading as a whole then you are ready to potentially change your life. In the upcoming chapters we will go over other ways to make large profits but why not add trading to your financial arsenal?

Main lessons from chapter 1:

. Use leverage to propel your profits

. Only risk what you can afford to lose

. Risk it until you make it

. Try to make unemotional decisions by suppressing your amygdala

. Only invest/trade in what you understand

CHAPTER 2: APRIL

THE FINANCE FIASCO

My April was split into three distinct sections. The spending spree, the savings spree, and the end of my active trading career. I'll let you guess which one came first.

If you guessed savings spree, well you would be wrong. In typical gen Z fashion, as from the 2nd of April, I set about spending my net worth as fast as possible. A time in my life which I would later come to regret but thinking back it was something that had to happen for me to learn the value of money. Let's get started.
Of course in April lockdown was happening all over the UK. Nobody was allowed to leave the house, except for essential workers or when people exercised. It was a crazy time to be alive and goes without saying that it was just plain boring. My attention went away from the stock market and towards what I could buy, which at the time was pretty much anything I wanted. My only option was to shop online and wait for my items to arrive in the mail. I bought a selection of clothes and shoes even though I would claim that I did not care

about fashion. That was simply not true. After two days of scouring the internet, I had a completely new wardrobe, I had spent thousands of pounds on what I now consider meaningless junk that I do not even wear because I am embarrassed at how much I spent. After two days of endless spending, I turned my attention to what I could purchase as an investment. Briefly looking at artwork but what would an 18-year-old do with a painting? You should invest in what you are passionate about, for me I had no appreciation for art so avoided it altogether and searched the web further to find that watches could potentially be a worthwhile investment. Watches were my kryptonite. I enjoyed searching the internet for different watch brands and deciding which I would buy when I was older and had my full-time job. I saw them as an investment that was going to gain value in the future, this is not always true. Only the high-end watches appreciate, the mid-low priced watches usually just hold their value or sometimes depreciate. Like gold or other commodities (physical assets). At the time I thought I was being clever with my money and 'investing' in a medium-priced watch, however, I was really just buying the watch to appear rich. It boosted my ego which by this time was already sky-high. I went for the cheapest mid-end watch on the market at the time and had it delivered to my house. There was just one problem, my parents. I did not want them to see the watch, they still couldn't know my financial situation, I hated the thought of me being made to give my money away for petty reasons, knowing this I stayed quiet whenever the subject of money came to the dinner table. I still had all of my expenses covered by my parents and wanted to keep it that way. If they saw a shiny, new watch on my wrist then questions would be asked. I felt like a secret agent, I needed to make sure I intercepted the package before my parents saw, then hide the box (with the watch inside). I was therefore buying a watch which I would never wear and hardly even look at. It was a pointless purchase but non the less bought the watch. In my 18 years, this is my worst purchase and probably will be for a very long time. At least with the clothes and shoes, I was getting more than one item. The problem with most young people is that they spend their money as soon as they get it from work, birthdays, or Christmas. If you take care of your money then your money will take care of you. I was no exception, you see me spend far too much money in early April just a few weeks after making the money. There are intelligent places to put your money. Clothes, shoes, and watches are not intelligent places. Later in the Gen Z's Rags to Riches handbook, I show you how to invest for the long-term and how to delegate your income, something that your future self will thank you for in years to come.

On the 6th of April, my spending spree was over. In total had spent thousands on various items, feeling ashamed of myself I naively assumed I could make the money back by trading. After my last trading experience, this was not an option, I had no intention of stepping back into the high-pressure world of trading. I was wrong, I would step back into the ring one more time but we will soon get to that.

Ever since I started trading I had forgotten the value of money, before I would have been happy with just a small part-time salary. I had just spent that on a pair of shoes. Realising the value of money early in life is useful, it sounds obvious but otherwise, you just continue to spend, spend, and spend some more. It can take years to save a substantial amount of money and only 5 minutes to spend it. Regardless of how much you earn, whether a salary or just money from family, I urge you to save at least 10% each month. It feels good to see your accounts build up and it makes a person more independent, something every gen Z wants. It took 1 month and 6 days for me to see that I was treating money like I had an unlimited amount and that I cared too much about other people's opinions. Wearing a nice watch, clothes and shoes only made me more self-conscious and once again allowed my amygdala to take over. I refused to stay in this anxious state, I was determined to make a change.

Embarking on a journey to change both my mindset and spending habits would take a lot of work and patience. We have nearly infinite resources at our disposal, the internet gave us sites such as YouTube, Amazon, and a variety of other sources only a few clicks away. It is amazing. For me, I needed more knowledge about investing and personal finance. Knowing only one way to make money wasn't enough, I needed to know how to save and invest. I started on YouTube which is, in my opinion, the best place to quickly obtain knowledge through visual learning, perfect for a gen Z. My expenses and spending habits needed to change first. This is true for most people because it is usually overlooked, if you want more money then spend less. It's that simple. My expenses included nearly a dozen subscriptions that took money out of my bank account every month, these included sites such as Netflix and Xbox. It may sound petty but these subscriptions add up and over time can potentially take hundreds out of your account each month, you need to ask yourself do I really need this and how often do I use it? Having zero subscriptions, I take it to the extreme but if I subscribe to one site then I am tempted by another and another so not bothering seems the best solution. I live frugally and well below my means, this is a great way to live since you can maximise profits and keep expenses as low as possible.

Next on the list was my spending habits. To stop me from buying pretty much anything I could get my hands on I needed more than just educational videos, which lead me to search for books. I bought all the go-to finance books by huge names such as Tony Robbins, Ray Dalio, and Richard Branson. I consider these guys my idols, they seemingly had all the money in the world but still wanted to give away their knowledge. They taught me to spend money on what I find important and for me, that was building my wealth as a gen Z, after becoming wealthy enough I would educate other people as I am doing in 'The gen Z's Rags to Riches Handbook'. My spending problem could be easily solved. Stop spending. For the rest of April, I did not spend a penny, it was as if I was broke. I put aside some money for trading in the future when I was ready, then the rest of my money went into a savings account, where the money could earn interest. Interest seems insignificant but with high amounts of money, it can make a real difference. If you are holding a low amount of money in a savings account then you need to concentrate on increasing your income. I am not going to lie to you, increasing income can be hard if you are in a job. Often a company does not have any promotions or extra hours for offer. Try to concentrate more on non-work income such as trading and investing. Build some revenue streams. This type of income is called passive income, basically money you earn with very little effort. Passive income comes in many forms such as rental income, dividends, buying and selling stocks/commodities, royalties, and interest.

My main source of passive income in April was interest, later in the handbook, I take you through how to increase your passive income by investing. My savings account offered 0.15% interest per month so I would receive 0.15% of my total balance paid back to me as a thank you from the bank. Viewing this as my income I searched through my library of books looking for a method to maximise my finances.

April the 16th, a day of what seemed like an endless search I found a personal finance technique called the 50/30/20. This means delegating my income as follows:

50% - expenses
30% - fun
20% - save/invest

The 50/30/20 technique is great if you have a fixed salary, it gives you a map of where to put your money but for me, I had no expenses. On April the 17th I made my own technique, a technique I still use today, the 90/10 rule. As a gen Z I still do not have many expenses so can save more, in April my expenses were still zero. This gave me a great opportunity to build my wealth, if your expenses are low then save as much possible for later life.

Over the last 17 days, my mindset had changed completely, having gone from being a compulsive spender to being extremely frugal. It had once again been a financial rollercoaster, I could not catch a break! On April the 18th I was caught by a news story while walking through the lounge in my house, once again there was a dreaded headline 'oil crash'. I was intrigued. My last experience with oil was the worst of my life. I had lost an unfathomable amount of money. Needless to say, I approached trading with much more caution now. I opened my trading account just to look at how the oil index had performed over the past few days. Surely enough, oil was collapsing. Having put aside the money for trading, would I take the leap one last time? I could not make this decision on my own, leading me to call George once again. We discussed for a full hour and had finally reached a decision, a decision which would once again change my life. I was back in the game, I made a deal with myself just to trade oil while it was so volatile. After oil calmed I would stop and I did. Having not traded since.

The phone call with George finished at 2 pm and I deposited my funds. Once again presented with the options of puts and calls or short and buy. I remembered that even when an instrument is crashing it can still have a dead cat bounce, how could I forget? With leverage at 1:50, I decided to buy as many puts as possible. Gambling and gambling big. I wanted to hold overnight. Anxious nights now seemed routine when trading but the night of April the 18th was certainly the worst and I was seriously questioning my decision. I had just learned how to save money and yet I was risking a minimum of £3,000 on an overnight trade.....ON PUTS. Waiting anxiously for the market to open on April the 19th I had flashbacks to a month before when it had gone wrong, sat on the step in front of my house and had such negative thoughts.

1 am showed on my phone, 'put +200%' the oil index had dropped 15% at market open. I opened my phone as fast as possible and closed my trade. I was overcome

with emotions, the risk paid off. Collapsing to the floor close to tears, I was more relieved than happy. I made the mistake of risking far too much money but had got lucky. My trading career had come to an explosive end. Again making a great return, in total 500% on my capital.

It had been a rollercoaster over the last 2 months and truthfully I was glad it was over. Trading is great but after so much anxiety and pressure, it starts to take a toll on both the mind and body.

That following week I cashed out my profits and delegated them with my 90/10 rule. 90% savings and 10% fun. Deciding to save all the money since I did not see the point in spending so much after recently buying what seemed like countless pieces of clothing. I decided to take the following week off, doing what most gen Z kids do when they are having a break, I watched Netflix. 20 movies and 5 series over the week (far too much I know), I needed to get some exercise. I welcomed the laziness and it was a great way to detox from the stress of trading. What is life without a little laziness?

Everyone needs a break. When I was 16 I worked as a lifeguard. This part-time job took up my weekend while I was studying all week at college. I did not have a day off and hated it. This is why passive income is so important, you can earn money while your asleep, with zero effort you just buy and hold. Patience is the key, ultimately the more passive income you have the less you need to work.

As the end of April was fast approaching I focused my attention on improving my mindset, everybody has seen a quote from the internet, been inspired then forgotten about it the next day. I was looking for a state of mind where I could be constantly motivated because if you are rich in the mind eventually you will be rich in the bank, a simple equation. After searching around I found a philosophy called Stoicism, I am not going to go into detail about the philosophy but especially as a gen Z it can be a great mental tool to have. It is the philosophy of not focusing on what you can't control therefore you do not focus on what people are thinking or how they act, you can't control this so why waste energy trying. You should focus on what matters and for me that was entering May with a rich mindset, to avoid the mistakes I made in April and to increase my wealth by investing my new profits for the long-term.

Summary of chapter 2:

I started April by spending as much as possible on items such as clothes, shoes, and even a watch. I later learned the value of money and came to the realisation I was spending far too much. I set out on a mission to learn about personal finance, to cut down my expenses, and get my spending to practically zero. I used interest as a form of passive income and learned the 50/30/20 rule, giving me control over my money. I then decided to use my remaining balance to trade with, made a large (high risk) trade and profited highly. Hating the stress of trading I ended my trading career abruptly. I then worked on my mindset while taking a break through the rest of April where I learned the ancient philosophy, Stoicism. April was just as crazy as March, not on a financial scale but a mental scale. The main lesson to take away from April is that no matter how much money you have, every penny needs to be valued, and learning how to delegate your income is an invaluable skill to have.

Main lessons from chapter 2:

. Learn the value of money early

. Do not care about others opinions

. Make sure to delegate your finances (50/30/20 rule)

. Work for cashflow/passive income (more on this in May/June)

. The fastest way to have more money is to cut some of your expenses

. Do not focus on what you can't control

CHAPTER 3: MAY

THE INVESTING ESCAPADE

Compound interest, the most powerful force in the universe. Depending on your age compound interest can be your best friend because of exponential growth. The concept that money will grow (by itself) faster and faster over time. To show you how powerful compound interest can be I am going to use 3 examples:

If you invested £1000 into an investment with a 10% return each year for 60 years, you would end up with £304,481.64

If you invested £10,000 into an investment with a 10% return each year for 60 years, you would end up with £3,044,816.40

If you invested £100,000 into an investment with a 10% return each year for 60 years, you would end up with £30,448,163.95

As you can see the original amounts compounded into truly staggering amounts. Yes, 60 years is a long time but the more money you invest the faster the exponential growth and the more your money compounds. People often use the analogy of a snowball rolling down a hill, as the snowball rolls it picks up more snow and gradually rolls faster until the snowball is racing down that hill. In May I discovered the best ways to achieve a good rate of compound interest and on May the 2nd discovered Vanguard. My life would never be the same.

Vanguard is one of many long term investing sites that offer various products, designed to gradually build wealth over the long term. On the morning of May the 2nd I was reading a book on long term investing, a book by Tony Robbins. He had interviewed the greatest minds in finance and compiled this advice into just 200 pages. I hated reading long books since I would constantly practice and research what the book would say, with so many pages I found my mind constantly wandering. This is the reason the gen Z's Rags to Riches handbook is just 5 chapters, with my experiences being summed up and down to the point. Perfect for any gen Z on the go. The Tony Robbins book cycled through the advantages of investing in the long term, regardless of how the market performs. As a trader this was a revelation, I was used to trading a volatile market not holding onto the stock for years. The statistics show that people who just buy and hold beat the people who try to time the stock market by buying and selling in a short amount of time. I understood the concept, just hold on. This was great info but I had no idea what to actually buy.

Previously I had traded index funds. Index funds track the performance of a group of companies, when a company underperforms it is switched with a better one. They are essentially risk-free and can be a great investment. I had never contemplated that I could buy a part of an index fund and own stocks in many of these great companies. Companies such as Microsoft, Apple, and Netflix. Every gen Z has purchased something from these companies and it is definitely cool to own part of them, in essence, you are paying yourself.

As May the 2nd was coming to a close I had finished my research and decided I should allocate most of my money to Vanguard, more specifically the S&P 500 index fund. The S&P 500 index fund tracks the performance of the 500 largest companies in the US, as you buy a share of this fund you are owning part of corporate America. Capitalism at its finest, as America grows your net worth grows too. There are countless index funds available, pick the one that suits you and start investing. Just make sure you do your research, this handbook is a great place to start.

The following week I learned some different ways of how to maximise my returns with Vanguard, I will go through 3 that are the most effective over the long term:

. Lump-sum investing (maintaining/building wealth)

. Pound cost averaging (building wealth)

. Using an ISA (building wealth while being tax-efficient)

They may sound complicated, believe me, I thought so in May, they are however easy to implement and I will show you exactly how.

Let's start with lump-sum investing. This style of investing is great if you are starting with a large amount of money, which I understand as gen Z's is unlikely, after all I started with just £400. This needs to be in here just because of its simplicity. As I talked about before with buying and holding. Lump-sum investing is exactly that, you use a large amount of money to buy a big chunk of an index fund (as I did). By doing this you can keep your wealth in a safe place, while also achieving an average 8-10% return per year (average return of the S&P 500). Great returns with little risk, no anxious nights just a relaxing investing experience. As well as the returns of the index fund you also receive dividends from the companies you now own which you can reinvest to further maximise returns. With these dividends you could also potentially retire, I know as a gen Z retirement seems a million miles away but the sobering reality is that it will eventually come. Of course you want to be financially free! If your account builds to, for example, £5,000,000 over 40 years, a dividend of 2.4% would bring you £120,000 a year. To me that seems like a great retirement, your account still also grows with a yearly return therefore increasing your yearly dividend. This retirement tactic works with all 3 methods of investing but obviously works the best when starting with a large amount. It is a great way to have an early retirement.

The next method is the pound cost averaging method, which works best if you have fixed income such as a salary. Remember the delegation method from chapter 2? The idea that you split your income as 50% expenses,

30% fun, and 20% savings. The section delegated to saving and building your wealth can also be used to invest some of your salary. Each payday you put away (for example 10%) and invest in an index fund. Over time with compound interest and your savings the account will gradually grow faster and faster until your salary is no longer needed. This method is the best out there, especially for the average person working a job. View your investing account as a savings account, do not be scared to invest, you can not be financially free without a little risk. To recap then, pound cost averaging is putting a section of your fixed income (salary) towards building your position in an index fund such as the S&P 500 on Vanguard.

The final method I am going to cover before moving on to buying individual companies is the ISA method. As I discovered on May the 10th an ISA is an account that has tax benefits, by using an ISA you pay 0% tax on profits. There is a catch. The ISA account has a limit of £20,000 per year. For most people just investing 10/20% of their salary, this is perfect because they will not reach the allowance within the current tax year. Meaning if a person wanted to sell some of their index fund they would be charged no tax, opposed to a normal account having to pay capital gains tax on their profits (10-20% in the UK). Therefore then an ISA account should be a consideration for people with a salary and are unable to invest a lump-sum. The pound cost averaging method can be used with an ISA account to maximise profits over the long term while also reducing tax, the perfect combo if your planning to invest less than £20,000. All 3 methods are proven strategies to build wealth over the long term, choose which is best suited for you and get investing!

By May the 11th I had taken full advantage of my investing account and was heavily invested in the S&P 500. I could not shake the feeling however that I could achieve more than 10% per year and try to outperform the market, something that many people try and most fail. Which is why index fund investing is so attractive. My idol Warren Buffet has achieved a better average return than the market over his lifetime and created a huge amount of wealth by doing so. At the age of 90 Buffet has a net worth of around $77 billion, that's b.... for billion. My best chance of achieving this kind of extraordinary wealth was not through an index fund but through buying individual stocks, I put aside around 5% of my cash and in typical gen Z fashion procrastinated for 2 days. Then started my research.

I found that buying stocks in individual companies is an unbelievably complex subject, you have limited information about a company and it introduces much more risk. What if the company closed down? What if the company took on to much debt and went bankrupt? All these questions were rushing through my head. I had started to study Buffet's annual shareholder meetings, where he answered questions from everyday investors, like you and me. He had the philosophy that when you find a company that fits your preferences then you should buy and hold, just like an index fund. He held companies such as Coca-Cola and Apple, they were giants in the corporate world. When Buffet invested in these companies they were undervalued at the time, meaning he naturally achieved higher returns when more and more people bought the stock. My thought process on the weekend of May the 16th/17th was that I needed to find companies that were undervalued which just after a market crash turns out to be very easy. Throughout March, April, and May stocks had fallen dramatically in value, some had bounced back strong but most were generally still very cheap. I was spoilt for choice. Even though most companies were now brilliantly cheap I still had to consider 3 main factors when choosing each stock:

. Amount of debt

. Retained earnings

. Amount of cash (how long the company can survive without business)

I am going to give a brief introduction to the 3 factors which can make a stock look attractive. Let's start with the amount of debt. Debt shows up on what is called a balance sheet (a balance sheet shows a companies assets, liabilities, and shareholders equity). The more debt a company takes on generally the less attractive the stock, however, a company may take on more debt when trying to, for example, build more property or further grow the company. The profit margin decreases when more long/short term debt is used by the company so it is always a great idea to research the companies plans and to discover what the debt is being used for. Debt also needs to be compared to assets, a company may have high amounts of long term debt but also a large stack of cash but more on cash to debt later. It is most important then to understand why the company is taking on debt, if it is not using debt productively then it is probably a poor investment. Retained earnings are found on the shareholder's equity section of the balance sheet is possibly the most important factor when choosing a company to invest in. Retained earnings are profits that are reinvested back into the company. If the retained earnings in a company have grown year over year, it shows that the company is improving and productively using their profits. If the retained earnings are decreasing or staying the same then the company could be stagnating and likely profiting less. Meaning it may not be the best investment. Surely you want to invest in a company that is using higher profits to reinvest in itself?

Finally, I will cover the amount of cash. Which companies can survive in a pandemic or other extreme circumstances? The companies with cash and plenty of it. If a company is in trouble then it can finance the company and take on debt. Debt eats up cash but if a company builds its cash stores, then it can pay off more debt and survive without business for longer periods. If a company has a lot of cash lying around then they can also take advantage of opportunities when they arrive, a company with no cash would need to take on more debt to take advantage of some great opportunities. This decreases the profit margin and the retained earnings of the company making it a less attractive investment. Just as leverage was king in trading, cash is king in the corporate world.

On May the 18th I had this brief understanding of how to invest in individual companies, I searched all day for the perfect company to invest in. Thinking back to March I had the idea of actually investing in one of my trading brokerages, plus 500. The company had virtually no debt and had been growing its retained earnings over the past 4 years. Everything I was looking for. Another reason that Plus 500 would be a great investment is that I completely understood how the company operated, having used it in March and April. Plus 500 had dropped in price from £20.40 per share in August of 2018 down to £5.00 per share in April of 2019 and had been climbing in price since. The company had seen a big boost in earnings since more people had started to trade stocks on the site. It peaked my interest.

I took a day to ponder and decided that Plus500 was a great investment so I bought many shares in the company, in essence, I was now an owner of a huge trading company, it felt awesome! Everyone that lost money trading would be generating money for me and I would receive the money in the form of dividends each year. I had created another revenue stream, which gave me more passive income, both the stock price and dividends would increase my wealth each year. I was taking full advantage of the compound interest by investing in both index funds and individual stocks, creating a financial foundation for myself. I did something that every Tom, Dick, and Harry* can do, remember I was just an average kid that got £400 for his birthday. There are many apps/websites to use if you are interested in buying shares in individual companies, just be careful that you are investing and not trading. There is a huge difference especially since trading is leveraged, do not make that mistake it can be very costly.

The last ten days of May I was reading relentlessly. As my financial arsenal increased I was able to differentiate between an attractive investment and one which was sub-par, I spent 2 days investing in various companies such as Hollywood Bowling, Carnival cruise lines, and ITV. All companies had great reputations in their industries and had little competition. Cycling through the 3 factors I covered earlier in the chapter I found all 3 companies to fit the criteria and of course due to the pandemic the stock price had plummeted over the previous months, needless to say, I took the opportunity. Meaning by the end of May my wealth was in a variety of investments, I had money in a savings account (earning interest), was now heavily invested in an index fund and owned shares in 4 huge companies that were all paying me yearly dividends. I had however been interested in a computer trading account which I had seen advertised on an investment network. I had no idea what I was getting myself into. June would turn out to be the month of excitement, naivety and betrayal.

Tom, Dick and Harry* - English saying meaning 'everybody'

Summary of chapter 3:

May was a month full of education and growth. I learned the basics of compound interest and how to invest in index funds over the long term, creating sustainable wealth. I read about the various ways to invest via sites such as Vanguard, I optimised my profits by using the lump-sum method and reinvesting dividends. Later in May I also learned the basics of how to invest in individual stocks and chose 4 companies which were attractive investments, I started investing in individual companies to try and achieve higher returns resulting in a bigger boost in wealth. Something that most try but are unable to successfully do.

Main lessons from chapter 3:

. Compound interest is a great way to achieve long term wealth

. Index funds offer great returns and very little risk

. Lump-sum investing method

. Pound cost averaging method

. ISA investing method

. Achieve potentially higher returns from buying shares in individual companies

. Only invest when you understand how the company operates

. Debt factor

. Retained earnings factor

. Cash factor

CHAPTER 4: JUNE

THE COMPUTER CHICANERY

Complete. This is how I felt as June the 1st arrived. I had a solid foundation of knowledge with finance, was a saveaholic, a savvy investor, and an avid reader. I had gone through failure and overcome it. Making me a mature gen Z. As I later discovered, the good times never last whether the problem is health, financial, or relationship related. The bad times will always arrive. I constantly received emails from various business people wanting capital for their investments. There were plenty of real estate deals, stock purchases and start-up companies. I generally ignored most of the requests but enjoyed receiving them, it made me feel more professional as an investor. On June the 3rd I got an email which read:

Hello Jake,

We are looking for investors to invest in our company (which I will not disclose). We generate superior returns.

We have a track record of an average of 88% over 5 years of testing. We are looking to raise £500k.

The minimum investment is £5k.

Of course, this was only a section of the email but I am sure you get the idea. This company had averaged returns of 88%, which is extraordinary. Over 60 years if you invested only £5,000 with this kind of return you would end up with a total amount of £140,747,587,708,545,007,616.00.
A hilarious amount of money, in fact, a near-impossible amount of money over 60 years (starting with only £5000). The email grabbed my curiosity. Looking back I remember being pumped with adrenaline and was about to call the company after seeing the email, once again my amygdala was taking over and I was getting emotional. Just from a single email. Even though it was not me that was trading, the feeling of anxiety started resurfacing. I was once again on a money high.
I woke up June the 4th with a spring in my step. Bouncing around the house and doing the classic gen Z jiggle, something I had not done since March. Maybe this was a sign my life was circling back and I was about to hit another huge profit but this time through a high-tech trading robot. This time I had much more security through my other investments (index funds/stocks and a pile of cash earning interest) my view was that I had money to spare and that achieving a great return through trading would diversify my net income. I now viewed trading as a form of passive income, which I can say from experience is complete bullshit. Even though

trading requires no actual effort it takes a mental toll that lasts however long you trade for, as you saw in March when I went 2 days without sleep. This time I was using a trading robot, it required zero effort on my part but the same kind of mental fortitude.

The company traded a type of asset called cryptocurrency. Examples of cryptocurrencies are Bitcoin, Ethereum, and Ripple. They are another way to store money (just like gold), generally, during a market crash people want to store their wealth in assets other than stocks. Cryptocurrencies then receive a lot of attention and usually increase in value, they do not actually produce income like a stock/bond/index fund. A great example of when Bitcoin was given a large amount of speculation* was 2017. A bitcoin went from the value of 1.28 in early 2017 to highs of around 29.5 in December (2017). THAT IS A HUGE RETURN! The bitcoin surge was short-lived however and was followed by a crash, the high of 29.5 dropped down to 3.84 just one year later. The 2020 market crash was a clear indication that gold and bitcoin would once again surge in value, on June the 5th Bitcoin had a value of around 11.26 and climbing because people had moved away from stocks and wanted a secure place to store their wealth.

I did not care about whether Bitcoin increased or decreased in value over the long term, it was irrelevant since I was planning to use a trading robot to buy and sell bitcoins in a very short amount of time. The volatility was a good thing. I was still uneasy about contacting the company, I tried to imagine the huge returns on the capital. The reward was potentially huge. I neglected the potential downsides such as losing control of my money and the risk involved with allowing an account manager to experiment with different levels of risk. Ultimately my main problem was the account manager, not the trading but we will get to that.

June the 8th I finally plucked up the courage to fork out some of my capital. After depositing the funds to the online website they gave me access to the web trader (where you can see the trades completed by the computer). Then receiving a call from an account manager. I was sat in my kitchen eating breakfast around 9 am, the usual gen Z iced coffee and cereal. I rushed over to the phone which was on the other side of the room next to the coffee machine and picked up my iPhone, it read 'London England' followed by an unfamiliar number. It was my account manager.

The conversation lasted approximately an hour. We talked about the condition of the current market, long-term investing, trading stocks and then finally bitcoin. I was in my element, finally there was somebody I could relate to. Most of my friends supported my adventures in finance but were clueless about the details, most young people are. Just by reading this book you are one step ahead. I asked the account manager about these apparent 'superior returns'. He described that the 2020 market crash had boosted the companies profits and they were having truly amazing returns on the initial investment. He complimented me on my success earlier in the year, of course, he was only trying to get my money but I still appreciated the attention. The phone call came to an end as we discussed the future of bitcoin, he believed bitcoin would once again return to its sky-high value of nearly 30. I was sceptical, fewer people trusted bitcoin after so many people got burned when the bitcoin bubble burst and plummeted back to single digits. I tried to be open-minded however and appreciated he had much more experience. We agreed on the amount of the initial deposit and said he would gear the trading robot to my account. All I had to do was sit back and relax, my specialty.

June the 9th I rolled out of bed, tired from a night of watching movies. My laptop was sitting on my desk next to my flask and air pods. I was hesitant to look at first but after 10 minutes realised that if I lost the money my life would be no different, I would eat the same things, wear the same clothes and live in the same house. Thinking like this can be beneficial however when the unlikely circumstance of losing the money you claim not to need actually happens, it can still be a heart-throbbing event especially with as much as thousands. As I covered in chapter 2 knowing the value of money from an early age can be invaluable. The truth was if I lost the money then my life would be different, as I learned later in the month. Logging on to the web trader, I could see the trades that took place in the last 12 hours. My balance had increased, the trading robot had produced a profit of 20% overnight, while I was asleep. I had the same sensation and excitement as I had in March. This was a great profit and in such a short amount of time, just one day! Again at 9:30am I had a call with my account manager. Describing how I felt about the performance of the trading robot, I said it was the future of finance. We talked for another 20 minutes and eventually arrived at the topic of using more capital, he wanted more money after just one day. This was the first red flag, I was trying to explain to him that my initial deposit was a substantial amount of money considering that just 3 months ago I only had £400 to my name. I understood that to achieve higher amounts of profit you needed more capital but refused to deposit more money and sell my other long-term investments. Finally he backed down and we moved on to talking about currencies.

I watched my profits increase all day long. Eating ice-cream, watching movies on Netflix, and later going for a jog (because I felt guilty about the ice-cream). By the end of June the 9th I spent some time adding up my net worth and checking the performance of my companies. My long term stocks had grown in value by an average of 50%, my index funds were recovering strongly and I still had a small amount of cash in a high-interest savings account. I had never actually spent the time to sit down and work out my net worth. I knew I achieved a sky-high return in 2020 but didn't realise I was sitting on such an overwhelming amount. Now I had a trading robot doing the hard work for me, life in early June could not have been better.

Humble. This is how I tried to act at all times after my highly arrogant spell in April, determined not to repeat the same mistakes as the past. One week went by and I watched my account balance increase exponentially, each new day came with a new profit. We had a call scheduled on Friday, I was planning on thanking the account manager. My account by Friday morning had reached almost double my starting balance in just one week. A profit of thousands in just 5 days.

As I readied myself for the call I received an email:

Hello Jake

Let me know when the best time to call you.

The call was already arranged to be on Friday, what was the problem? I replied promptly, stating that we had already arranged the call for Friday morning. My friends had warned me (with their limited knowledge) about the risks that came with using an outside source to control my money, their words were transparent. I would not go to them for advice about money so why would I care about their opinions on the matter. I was not being open-minded, which is now one of my principles. Living with principles can be a really great thing to consider, they allow you to avoid mistakes. Every bad situation has a lesson behind it, life is pointless if you just keep repeating the mistakes of the past. There will be a section in the back of the handbook to write your own principles, here are my principles as an example:

1. Do not focus on what you can't control
- What people think
- Market volatility
- illness

2. Do not buy something (non-necessity) unless you can buy 10
- Money from the fun account
- Not overall amount

3. Do not make decisions from impulse
- Spontaneous purchases
- Spontaneous investments

4. Always remember, the goals will lead you to the end goal
- Goals act as stepping stones

- Always strive to reach them

5. Make every big decision with the end goal in mind
- Living costs
- Apartment buys
- Apartment rents

6. Plan every possible outcome of a situation
- Be an obsessive planner

7. Live as a problem solver
- Every goal and dream is just a problem
- Waiting to be solved

8. Spend a lot on items used for investing and income
- Laptops
- books

9. Do each step to the goal as relentlessly as possibly
- Burning ambition

10. Be open minded when confronted with an argument
- Try not to be always right, if your probably wrong

These principles have stopped me from making the same mistakes time and time again. Such as my 'buy 10' principle. I do not buy anything unless I can buy 10 items (money from the fun account). It stops me from overspending, as a gen Z with a slight shopping addiction this is debatably my most important principle.

The account manager needed a principle to have better punctuality to calls. My suspicion started at this point, have I potentially just given money away? My mind was ticking away. The combination of an unprofessional account manager and my friend's opinions started to take effect. I jumped into action and tried calling. Adamant on getting more information, all the while doubting the profits were even real in the first place. Certain I was getting played I could see a future principle revealing itself. After hours of calling on Friday I had no response, I called the helpdesk at the company, still no response. Ask yourself what you would do in this situation? I consider my next move a stroke of genius but that is just one gen Z's opinion.

June the 15th dawned, the day of my cunning plan to expose the company. I decided to make a new account using a different email and different phone number (since at this time I had invested in a second phone for business calls). My other phone was constantly being flooded with meaningless notifications, something that most young people experience. If you are a person who is always on calls with work or maybe you own your own company and need to talk to your employees, a business phone is life-changing. I was called soon after making an account by a secretary at the company (the same process I went through a week ago), claiming I was a potential investor, I was playing detective. After a short while, I was put through to an account manager and waited on hold. I had no idea what to say at this point, would it be the same account manager? It was irrelevant, I had to be ruthless and find out what the situation was. After 5 minutes of listening to a soothing Spanish guitar (on hold) I heard a beep then an eastern European voice.

It was a different account manager. I calmly explained my situation but he seemed almost angry with me, as though his time was being wasted. My amygdala was slowly taking over as I listened to him talk about market exposure, only thinking about how I had probably lost money. I interrupted him and asked if his company was a scam, of course he replied no. What more could I do? Leaving me with only one option to ask for a withdrawal. I was trying to be patient with his tedious conversation, finally I got around to asking him for the withdrawal. 'I will talk to the financial department' he said hesitantly. It seemed redundant but I was content with waiting a while, I was a patient person after all. I suppressed my amygdala and gave myself a pat on the back, having had stood up for myself.

I thought that was the end of the trading robot and the new chapter on my life was about to begin. A week went by while I waited to hear more information about my withdrawal. I thought I had matured enough not to fall for financial scams or to be tricked into a 'too good to be true situation' but was clearly wrong. I still had so much to learn. By reading this handbook you can see my successes but much more importantly my mistakes, only you should control your money. No matter how good the opportunity seems.

I was sat in my office at home, surfing the web and listening to music. A gen Z on the internet and listening to music, who would have thought haha? My music suddenly stopped and my phone started to vibrate. The name on the screen said unknown and the location, London England, this was the trading company! I expected more information about my withdrawal request and the opportunity to be refunded my money.

I'll let you guess who was on the other end of the phone...

It was my original account manager, he had called me by accident. What a strange series of events. I set upon quizzing him about why he had ignored my emails and calls after taking my money and cheekily asking for more. He was stuck for answers, I was crucifying him. He had taken advantage of an 18-year-old but this gen Z was not going to just lie down. As you saw in my principles, I have a principle about my goals:

9. Do each step to the goal as relentlessly as possibly
•   Burning ambition

I had financial goals I wanted to achieve by the end of 2020. Losing thousands did not fit into the mantra. I had to be relentless. During the call it hit me that no matter what was said he was still in control, I was powerless and had been ever since I deposited the money earlier in the month. No matter how much wealth you have life still puts you in situations where you have zero control, only this situation was here because of my naivety. I would never forget this lesson, since June I have tried to perform business activities as morally as possible. As though all of my actions would be on the front page of the newspaper and would be seen by my grandparents, I would want them to be proud. The account manager was certainly not operating from a moral standpoint, he ended the phone call with a now-familiar 'I will talk to the financial department'. Is this financial department deaf? Now, whenever I see anybody else who has been burned in the same way I can relate to them on a deeper level. You can not control how other people act but you can control how you think about the way they act, learning from each situation.

Nothing was going my way in June, I eventually received my deposit after weeks of calling, ending up not even getting the profits the robot achieved. I am however grateful that June happened. The month taught me to be a more moral person in business and life. I had hated the way that the trading company operated, which lead me to wonder how they stayed in business. As July was coming closer I had my sights on my most ambitious venture yet and the final chapter of my 5-month journey, founding my own company. Rivington Financials Ltd.

Speculation* - the purchase of an asset with the hopes it will gain in value

Summary of chapter 4:

I started June being excited about the opportunity that the trading company offered, which ended up being to good to be true. Learning this gave me an insight into how a company should be operated and allowed me to make a new principle based on being an honest person. I learned that you need to be very careful where you put your money and to always be in control. If you are in control then you can get out at anytime which decreases the risk dramatically.

Main lessons from chapter 4

. Always be in control of your money

. Never believe everything you read

. Make principles to avoid making previous mistakes

. Remember that good times never last

. Be open-minded when listening to people

. Take peoples advice into consideration rega

CHAPTER 5: JULY

THE COMPANY CONSUMMATION

Branson, Buffet, Musk, Gates, Zuckerberg, Bezos, and Jack Ma. What do all these guys have in common (other than being incredibly wealthy)? They all own companies. To me, owning a company is a gateway to potentially vast amounts of wealth. As an employee there is only so far a person can go until they have reached the top of the ladder, even people such as lawyers, doctors and bankers. I was in awe of big company owners, how could somebody not be inspired by the Rags to Riches stories of, for example, Jack Ma. He was poor and jobless at a young age. Ma experienced more rejection than most of us ever will, he was rejected from 30 jobs where he lived. Even at KFC Ma was the only person out of 24 people to be rejected, he was also rejected from Harvard 10 times and rejected from the police. It goes without saying he heard the word "no" a lot. Through resilience, he was able to overcome his constant rejections and build a company. That company is Alibaba and now has a net worth of $84 billion giving Ma a personal net worth of $54 billion, making him the richest man in China. He is an incredibly inspirational character and has a motto of "if you don't do it nothings possible". On July the 1st I decided to take Ma's advice and made the decision I was going to form a company.

There was just one problem, I was clueless and had no idea how to operate or even make a company. What would my company do? What are my responsibilities as a director? What are the downsides? I set a goal to form the company by the end of July with a solid business plan. A goal worth working for!

My first consideration was the downside of forming the company. When starting anything new it is pivotal that you check what could go wrong, a lesson from June, if the risk is more than the reward then its obviously a mistake. Since I was going to be the director I had no downside financially unless my capital used my personal money. The company is classed as a separate entity meaning if the company needs to close or default due to debt, I would not need to repay the debt with my personal wealth. Learning this on July the 2nd was great, it gave me more courage because I knew there was less risk. It had been my main concern, I was planning to jump into the corporate ocean headfirst and having no idea how to swim. The relief that came with 'limited liability' was important going forward. Overall then the downside was virtually zero, I would do everything in my power to not use my own money. I needed more finance options, my only option was my investment network.

On July the 3rd I logged into my investment network. The month before, I had a horrible experience with the network after being approached by the trading company but this time was not an investor. For the first

time in my life, I was an entrepreneur. In the morning I
had to consider the downside with getting an investor
on board and the complications with asking for
professional help/money. Was I willing to give part of
my soon-to-be-formed company away? The answer was
a strong no but I still needed the start-up capital,
spending all day looking at different options I came
across a corporate loan with a great interest rate of just
6%. As I covered in chapter 3 a company can take on
debt when it is trying to grow and evolve. The debt did
add pressure for the company to succeed but I was
confident I would come up with a great idea. Jotting
down the loan company on the infamous yellow legal
pad I carried on with what seemed like an endless list of
considerations before the company incorporation. At
least I had my financing options covered, preserving my
personal money.

On the weekend of July the 4th/5th I pondered on an
idea for the company. Concentrating my brainpower on
my strengths which by this time was stocks, index
funds, and trading. Having only 3 qualities was not ideal
and narrowed down my options but I was a gen Z on a
mission, determined to make it work. I had a burning
ambition to give the company a great start.

My first idea came to me while I was in the shower, a
strange place to be thinking about business I know but
it is the truth (a foundation which I wanted to build the
company on). The idea was that people would give their
capital to the company and I would invest for them,
using my knowledge in the stock market. In theory, the
idea was perfect because of the limited downside, I did
not even need a start-up loan.

That week I delved into the details of starting such a
company, in essence I was starting a hedge fund. A type

of company that pools its investor's capital together to produce higher profits (by investing in various companies). It was going to be an ambitious project for a teenager that was for sure, I was not the same kid that rushed home to play Xbox after school, I was soon going to be a company owner. While other gen Z's used their time to procrastinate I used my time productively and it felt great. I embraced the prestige and continued with my research. On Friday the 10th I contacted the FCA -Financial Conduct Authority- getting details on how to start the company, including fees I had to pay for being registered with the agency. My plan was coming together, thinking I had it all figured out I waited for the email from the FCA agent.

The reply arrived on July the 13th. I opened up my laptop as fast as possible, excited about the prospects of potentially starting an investing company. I wanted a company with the ability to scale and build into a success, viewing a hedge fund as the best way to do this since I already had a little experience in the stock market. My stocks had increased in value while using my personal capital why could I not do the same with other people's capital? Then in what I consider another defining moment of my life, read the email. What seemed like a solid foundation for a company came crumbling down after I saw the fee arrangement. The FCA had said the company had to pay tens of thousands in fees before the company even started investing and using people's capital. My idea was simply just not possible, I did not have the experience to raise that kind of capital and did not want to take on a large amount of debt as soon as the company was incorporated. This was my dream and it was crushed with just one email, a steep learning curve. This is the day that I found out business can be cruel, I can only imagine how Jack Ma felt in his early years. Luckily I still had 20 days to come up with a business plan.....back to the drawing board. Starting a company is a complicated process, that's for sure but starting one without an idea was pointless. Over the last 3 months, I had read nearly 15 books all on personal finance and self-help, I classed reading as a passion. On July the 15th I stumbled across the idea of making my company a brand that sold self-help/finance books and knew just the type of people I wanted to help. Gen Z's!

The concept of using my company to create intellectual property came to me while I was on one of my weekly walks. Every week a selection of me and my friends would walk up a large steep hill (of course we classed it as a mountain), Rivington Pike. I tried to bring people with a good knowledge of business whether this was investing, accounting, branding or marketing. George (as you will remember from March) was great at marketing, we were people who had high ambitions and we bounced ideas off each other. A strange kind of ping pong. It is always great to surround yourself with like-minded people, be around people who are better than you and you will soon be at their standard. People knew that I had a good knowledge of investing and trading. People that wanted to increase their wealth started to spend more and more time with me. I started to be asked questions such as, how should I invest? Should I buy bitcoin? What would you do? I want to start trading and copy you? If I could just put all of the answers in one place, then it hit us halfway up the hill. I should write a book based on how young people can build wealth and how they could become rich. Finally, I had a company idea worth working towards, it had a purpose and a great meaning. Many gen Z's have buckets of ambition and intelligence but lack the knowledge to act on their talents, I wanted this book to provide just that. Still however I lacked a name for both the book and the company. I was in need of inspiration, July was taking a lot of brainpower and vision. At the top of the hill we looked down on our home town looking for our houses, trying to look under the endless blanket of fog. There was a lonely bench where we would sit and take in the serenity, we discussed the best places to walk. We both agreed on Rivington. Then as if by magic I just said: "Rivington that's it!" The company would from then on be called Rivington Financials Ltd. Breaking out the jiggle for the last time, I was elated, the name was meaningful and meant something to me. Rivington will always have a place in my heart, it was the perfect name.

By July the 16th I had a company name, financing options and a product. There was only one step left....actually naming the product. I thought back to earlier in the year. Having no money and my family struggling financially was tough, complaining was not an option however. Overcoming this and using my birthday money to make a small fortune was what I wanted to portray. If I could do it then anybody could. The book would be about my crazy experiences in the year 2020, they were unique and certainly had their ups and downs. It would be a roadmap to financial success showing both my successes and more importantly my failures. Being at a point where I could now help my parents financially gave me more purpose and showed that it is possible to change your life in such a short amount of time. I could summarise my experiences in one phrase 'gen Z's Rags to Riches'. The product name was born.

The end of the month was fast approaching, I had nearly achieved my goal ten days out. Goal setting is a big part of my life and I have come up with what other people have considered an effective system. The two main parts of my goal-setting system are having aims and time constraints. Time is considered the most important component of achieving your goals, it gives somebody a sense of urgency. I mostly set yearly or monthly goals, as you saw in my principles I work towards them relentlessly. Do not be too realistic with your goals, be ambitious and figure out the solution but try to not set absurdly high goals, you do not want to set yourself up for failure. Also having aims is pivotal to being a high achiever, aims should be bigger and better than the goals. Make them hard! If you manage to achieve your aims then you automatically achieve your goals. Your aims should also be more time conscious, give yourself less time. This will force you to wake up earlier and procrastinate less, something that most gen Z's struggle with. In summary then figure out exactly what you want, what are your goals? There will be a journal section (at the back of the handbook) to help you figure this out. Once you know what your goals are set your aims, these should harder, much harder. Once you know your aims and goals then put on time constraints. Give yourself less time to achieve your aims and a moderately hard amount of time for your goals. After these steps you are good to go, having monthly and yearly goals give you direction and with your principles, you will be unstoppable!

After seeing the poor quality of the trading company in the previous month I wanted some set values for my company, values me and my future team could live by. July the 20th was a day full of vision, imagining my company is 5 years' time. How would it look? I never came up with a set picture of a skyscraper office or thousands of employees, I came up with 3 simple rules. The first rule was that the company would be honest. Having a candid approach to selling our product would not only be more moral but we would soon be known for our honest view on modern finance. All of my experiences in this handbook have been 100% honest, in finance, that is hard to come by. The underlying message of our product is that anybody can use my concepts to better their lives, this is true all the way through the handbook. It's not about who you know it's about what you read.

The next rule was quality. I wanted to provide a quality product to customers, having high standards in everyday life transpired to this handbook. My experiences are given in as much detail as possible, made by a gen Z for other gen Z's. The concepts I used are proven techniques to build wealth, my trial and error approach showed just that.

The final rule was humility. If anybody on my team thought they were better then anybody else as a human being, they would be out. My attitude towards other people was obnoxious in March. Then life woke me up with some bad times which provided me with a large dose of humility. If a person lost their money in a scandal or bad investment I could now relate. They could still have amazing advice. We should not judge people by their position in society, we should judge people by their potential and willingness to do great things.

With my set values of honesty, quality and humility my company was virtually ready to go. Rivington Financials Ltd would not be operational until I gathered a team together but that could wait until after incorporation. I circled a date in my calendar, the date in which I would form my company. July the 31st, the end of my 5-month journey. Therefore I had 11 days to burn. What could a gen Z work on in 11 days?

Branding. How did I want my company to appear too the world? You have probably seen the company logo, it is on the cover of the book. I wanted the logo to be meaningful just like the name. I spent a full week working with software to try and create a simple yet elegant brand image. After hours of racking my brain, I came up with the logo you see dotted around the book. The crown-looking image represents not only a crown but the peaks on Rivington hill. The child-like 'gen Z' company message underneath shows the youthful side of the brand. After all we are only young once, we may as well have some fun. The branding for me was the most enjoyable part of the creation process, the creative side was completely new to me. Now if there is anything creative happening within the company I want to be the first to have a look and give my input.

By July the 31st the company had a complete start-up kit and was ready to be incorporated. This had been a month in the making. My dream/goal of owning a company was about to become a reality. I was building my legacy and the company was a great foundation. Life was great! I had used my £400 in March to kick-start my financial journey towards my end goal. I'm proud to be a gen Z born in the internet age, I was given no special advantages in life. Just initiative and a 'let's just do it' attitude, remember if there is no downside then why not try? You either succeed or learn.

Summary of chapter 5

July was all about the company. I started the month off by being inspired by Jack Ma, he taught me the advantages of a no downside situation. After making the decision to form my company I went over different ideas, settling on an intellectual based/self-help company based on finance. The rest of the month was mainly used to come up with names, values, a product, and finally a brand image. All of my past experiences lead me to make a company, I wouldn't have it any other way.

Main lessons from chapter 5

. If you don't do it nothings possible

. Forming a company should be a meaningful experience

. Have monthly/yearly goals

. Have time constraints on your monthly/yearly goals

. If there is no downside then why not try

AUTHORS SUMMARY

We live in the post-millennial age with social media all around us. Many people are scrolling through their life, focusing their energy on other people's lives. Social media and the internet can be amazing in so many ways, hey that is probably how you found out about this book! But it can also be unbelievably negative, it can lead to feelings of inadequacy about your life, FOMO, isolation, depression and most commonly anxiety. Instagram models can make you feel insecure about the way you look and rich people can make you feel worthless when they 'flex'. It is obvious that influencers need to use their status to promote self-worth and positivity but unfortunately, the world is full of people who just want to boost their egos, in turn making people envious. The reality is that the people seeming so beautiful, successful and rich were likely insecure at some point in their life and maybe still are. We as human beings can not control external factors such as how people act or how they look but we can control our minds and thoughts. Use inspiring people as motivation. People like Jack Ma and Warren Buffet, you do not so these multi-billionaires on Instagram sitting in vaults with piles of cash, you see them teaching people how to become better versions of themselves. I wrote the gen Z's Rags to Riches handbook to show that there is a way that 'normal everyday people' such as myself can become wealthy, it was not written to boost my ego or to impress other people. Whether you are starting with £4,000,000 or £400 like myself you can still make a difference and improve both your life and the peoples around you. Figure out what you want out of life early, if you want to spend all your time scrolling through other people's lives be my guest. If you want to be part of the 1% of gen Z's who have direction and purpose then you should:

1. Set your goals (monthly, yearly and your end goal)
2. Set your aims (can you beat your goals?)
3. Develop your principles (so then you do not repeat your mistakes)
4. Use my strategies to build wealth
5. Start your journey, making sure you always keep the end goal in mind

Use my 5-month journey as a guide. Avoid my mistakes and use my strategies to better your lives both emotionally and financially. Contact my team via the company email RivingtonFinancialsLtd@outlook.com, I want to know how this handbook has helped you and how you are planning to better yourself. Use the remaining two pages to plan out your ambitions.

As gen Z's we are the future, let's get it right!

Printed in Great Britain
by Amazon